D1413758

Blues for Bird

Blues for Bird

Martin Gray

Ekstasis Editions

Canadian Cataloguing in Publication Data

Gray, J.M. (James Martin)
Blues for Bird

Poem.
ISBN 0-921215-64-9

1. Parker, Charlie, 1920-1955—Poetry.

I. Title.
PS8563.R393B5 1993   C811'.54   C93-091771-5
PR9199.3.G739B5 1993

Copyright © Martin Gray, 1993
Cover art and design by Paul Jung.

Acknowledgements:
Portions of this long poem have been published in *Lines Review, Convolvulus, Ostinato* and *Thirteen*.

Published in 1993 by
Ekstasis Editions Canada Ltd.   **Ekstasis Editions**
Box 8474, Main Postal Outlet   Box 571
Victoria, B.C. V8W 3S1   Banff, Alberta T0L 0C0

for Ray and Lia Souster

Prefatory Note

Words cannot replace music, especially when it concerns a musical genius like Charlie Parker. His tunes and recordings will last as long as the compositions of Stravinsky or Bach. However words are the only way we can be biographical, and words can convey something of Bird's genius, his profoundly serious playfulness, his legendary generosity and his unparalleled musical skills in invention and performance. In relating some of the heights and depths in Bird's life within a narrative frame tone is the unifying element I have used, especially a comic tone. Although jazz itself is a serious business (and very serious indeed when it comes to technique and technical accomplishment) its pervading tone is parodic and comic. That is why in this narrative poem I have tried to maintain a pervasive comic tone throughout.

I would like to acknowledge four sources: Dizzy Gillespie with Al Fraser, *To Be Or Not To Bop*, Ira Gitler's *Swing to Bop*, Robert Reisner's *Bird: The Legend of Charlie Parker*, and Arthur Taylor's *Notes and Tones*. I thank Peter Enman for critical vigilance and an eagle editorial eye. The cover was designed and engraved by Paul Jung.

Music is your own experience, your thoughts, your wisdom. If you don't live it, it won't come out of your horn. They teach you there's a boundary line to music. But, man, there's no boundary line to art.

Civilization is a damned good thing, if somebody would try it.

Charlie Parker

Blues for Bird

I

Hear the tale of a Bird
his flights upon the horn
for almost twenty years
beginning at fifteen
ending at thirty-four.
Charlie was nicknamed 'Bird'
(so say jazz dictionaries)
because he did a rap
for his narcotic use.
'Bird' is a convict term
for someone who does time.

II

Jay McShann relates
another version of
how Charlie Parker gained
the nickname that he had
as in Nebraska State
their driver, Pat by name,
collided with a fowl
and Charlie called to him
'Hey Pat, back up this car!
You ran a yardbird down.
Let's stop and pick it up'
so Charlie got his chick
and reaching Lincoln said
'We ran a yardbird down
and he's still warm and fresh.
Can you cook him for me now?'
'Yardbird' he was from then,
most shortening it to 'Bird.'
He sure liked chicken fresh.
It was his favorite food.

III

Said Williams (Mary Lou)
a jazz piano queen
who knew Bird earliest
(they shared a neighborhood)
that Bird himself would bop
while still in his knee pants.
'In high school I first heard
an energetic horn
against the usual rhythm
when Bird invented Bop.'

IV

At thirteen he played both
the horn and clarinet
(his horn was baritone)
from all the lessons which
Alonzo Lewis gave
then two years later made
a dollar twenty five
for playing at a dance
(It was Thanksgiving Day)
was soon a regular.
A few months after this
studied with Carrie Powell
major and minor chords
seventh and diminished
and then he joined McShann.

V

One reason why McShann's
was such a happy band
was Charlie's membership.
McShann was wise enough
to give Bird latitude.
'If you let me play
with some happiness
you'll always have me blow
a few good notes for you'
is how Bird put his case.
His art and talent grew
whenever there was fun
till it was genius
infecting the whole band
and freeing up their play
to be spontaneous.

VI

When first Bird tried to show
all his talents off
he was too confident.
'I knew a tune or two
and played them as I could
jamming that first time
at the High Hat in K.C.
on Vine and 22nd.
The changes were not hard,
all numbers easy ones.
The reed men set a riff
only for the brass
and not behind the reeds.
No two horns would jam
together as they played.
I loafed until I tried
to double tempo on
a tune I thought I knew.
This tune was "Body and Soul."
Those who heard me play
laughed and jeered at me.
I went straight home and cried.
It took at least three months
before I played again.'

VII

Also in K.C.
upon a one night stand
he lacked an instrument,
one of a hundred times
he put in hock his sax
to raise some ready cash
so with an alto friend
arranged in turn to slip
quickly to the men's.
After the one had played
he leaned out from the sill
and passed on to his mate
the horn that they both played.
The two got through their gig
upon one instrument.

VIII

Whatever cash he made
immediately was spent
at first so he could chip
but soon it led to dope
at fifteen or sixteen
when he began to take
horse itself, the H
through older cats who said
if he wanted to play well
this was the stuff to take.
How was a poor young kid
to know the consequence?

IX

After the Ozark crash
which broke two of his ribs
(the bass man lost his life)
his boss a Selmer bought
its action faster than
all other kinds of horn.
Bird's fingers were a blur
but not the notes he blew.
Each single note was clear
and each one separate.

X

As Charlie never slept
he practised nights and days
living his music through
so all who passed his house
hearing his saxophone
warm mornings or cool nights
said to themselves 'That's Bird.
The man is woodshedding.'
Occasionally he'd doze
but did not rest in bed
was seated in a chair
and thus he seldom dreamt
except each time he played.

XI

While practising his horn
he did not play tunes through,
perhaps the first four bars
and scales and intervals
or holding on one note,
a part of loosening up.
The time to go all out
was when he took the stand.

XII

When Bird came to N.Y.C.
to further his career
washed dishes for his keep
and played there at Monroe's
but no one noticed him
lucky to get per night
forty or fifty cents
but if the place was packed
might make at least a fin.

XIII

'I used to quit each job
to go with Buster Smith.
He was my idol then.
But hearing at Monroe's
the latest style and hits
and that big city sound,
those romping trumpet men
Dizzie, Roy, Lips Page
and Charlie Shavers too,
man, they played everything!
I heard a trumpet cat,
Vic Coulson was his name
play things I'd never heard
and Pritchitt, tenor man.
Theirs was the kind of sound
made me leave McShann.'

XIV

'One night I jammed away
in Don Wall's chili house
bored continually
at all the stereotypes
persisting in the thought
that there was something else.
I heard it sound at times
but couldn't reach it yet.
Played "Cherokee" that night
and as I worked it through
I found that using just
the higher intervals
there within the chord
as a melodic line
with changes backing it
the thing I played I heard.
That night I came alive.'

XV

'Chicago '42
he played so brilliantly
but gigs were hard to find.
Everyone was scared
at talents such as his.
The country gone to war
had little time for jazz.
Almost a year went by
without a single gig
and very hard to find
someone who'd jam with him.
In two years he returned
and played but sixteen bars
and stopped the show. The house
was foyer to rafters full.
Unable to proceed
because of the applause
he had to do it all
again and yet again
before they let him go'
Art Blakey testified.

XVI

Often Bird had moods
as many artists have.
Said his tense manager
'I quit. You think you're God,
better than anyone else.'
A chastened Bird replied
'I was born like you
out of a pussy, man.'

XVII

Tutty Clarkin said
the first horn that Bird had
was held by rubber bands
and layers of cellophane.
The valves were always stuck,
reeds broken, badly chipped
and many leaky pads.
He held it out oblique.
That he could play at all
was a miracle.

XVIII

Late one night a key
fell broken from his horn
and taking up a spoon
he snapped it, fastening part
with chewing gum and tape
and blew through those small hours
with that same velvet tone
and little loss in sound.

XIX

'What is your best on wax?'
someone asked one day.
'Sorry, my best on wax
hasn't yet been made
but if you asked me for
what on wax is worst
I'd answer readily.
It is my "Lover Man."
I didn't wish release.
They waxed it just before
I was sentenced to
six months in hospital.'

XX

One evening in a bar
a youth came up to Bird.
'Man, you were wonderful!'
'This isn't my horn!' Bird cried,
'The B-sharp doesn't work,
the reed you hear all chewed.
How can you tell me that!'
Bravely the youth replied
'What has a guy to do
to pay a compliment?'
Parker was struck by this.
'Okay man okay
but this is not my horn.
The B-sharp doesn't work,
the reed you hear all chewed
but thanks, man, many thanks!'

XXI

To Tony Graye Bird was
'the kindest of the Titans.'
He met him following
a breathlessly fast solo
then much in awe he said
'I don't know what you're paid-—
I hope a buck each note.'

XXII

Art Blakey to a friend:
'You oughta hear this guy!'
'Can't outplay Willie Smith.'
'Man, oh yes he can.'

XXIII

Sidney Bechet who
was never known to praise
said to Charlie: 'Man,
those phrases that you make!'

XXIV

'Bird had amazing skill.
You could play a tune
and right away he'd play
a counter melody.
It came spontaneously'
said Trummy Young one time.

XXV

Earl Coleman worked two hours
to make two tapes. They failed.
He stopped to rest his pipes.
Then Charlie made two tunes.
'Bird's Nest' was the first
based on 'I Got Rhythm'—
Gershwin's ghost was pleased.
The second was 'Cool Blues'
then reeled off seven takes.
It took just half an hour.

XXVI

His name was Lester Young
but all just called him 'Prez'
short for the President.
Count Basie's was his band.
Parker said of him:
'Prez chuckled when I said
I was a fan of his
and have been so for years.
I sat beneath a stand
for hours to hear him play
because I loved the man.'

XXVII

Earl Coleman said of Bird
'His fingers were so sure
and he himself relaxed
he held a cigarette
between them when he played,
would puff it now and then,
his way of fingering
just like his idol, Prez.'

XXVIII

When Byas first heard Bird
his verdict was too harsh:
'You say nothing on your horn.'
Bird gave him a hard look
and told him to come outside
so Don and he went out.
Bird then pulled a knife
and Byas drew a blade.
Charlie glanced at him and smiled.
'I really think you'd cut'
and stowed his knife away.

XXIX

'You gotta go by Bird
if you ever want to swing'
was what Bud Powell affirmed.

XXX

'How I loved the way
Charlie Parker flew
all over his strong horn.
There ain't but few notes there.
In an octave eight
and just five sharps or flats.
He played so swift it seemed
he added several more'
reflected Sarah Vaughan.

XXXI

Bill Graham said of him
he could adopt a horn
of any type or make.
It didn't matter if
the reed was thick or thin
the sound he blew was his.
'He'd make a trombone play
just like an alto sax.'

XXXII

'The Monk runs deep' Bird said
and when Thelonius
played along with him
coming to chorus time
lost in his private world
from Monk there was no sound.
After a long delay
Monk struck a single note.
Bird leaned across to him.
'Crazy Monk' he said,
so warm in his response
to those from whom he'd learn.

XXXIII

The dancer Baby Lawrence
was seeking a new form,
improving dancing steps.
The first time he heard Bird
announced 'That form I've found.'

XXXIV

Her first name was Anita.
Her surname was O'Day.
She was a singing waitress
at Phillie's own Show Boat.
'When singing my third number
I heard an alto solo
propelling me, inspiring.
I went right through my piece
too scared to see who played
upon that saxophone.
When finally I finished
the man who played had gone.
Buddy de Franco led.
I asked him "Am I crazy?
Who *was* that?" Buddy answered:
"The man who played was Bird."
"It sure was" I replied
"because he flew out fast
as quick as he flew in."'

XXXV

In '49 Gene Roland
a Kenton trumpeter
started his own band
building it round Bird:
on baritone Bob Newman;
Al Cohn, Zoot Sims, Don Lamphere
and Charlie Kennedy
made up the tenor men;
Joe Maini was the alto;
lead trumpet Al Porcino;
on trombone Kenny Dorham,
Red Rodney, Eddie Burt.
Rehearsing for two weeks,
Bird steered and led superbly.
That was *the* dream band.

XXXVI

The format for arrangements
was every time the same.
The band played first ensemble
then Bird would play a solo
with the rhythm section
then the background would build up
section there by section
pianissimo
as softly first the saxes
trombones a little broader
the volume always building—
on top of that the trumpets.
By this time the whole room
vibrated with the music.
The volume of that sound
was near incredible
and right there at the summit
you heard Bird's raucous screaming
straight through the raging brass.

Their band was due to start
at Newark in two weeks.
Lord Buckley got the boss
to listen to their sound.
He liked it when he heard
but was frightened by its size
and fearful of the cost.
'I like your band' he said
'but it is far too big.
If you can knock it down
to just four men, I'll buy it.'
After that the band
vanished as snow in spring.
Bob Newman made a tape
upon a poor machine,
the only souvenir
of Bird's great orchestra
in existence for two weeks
but never played a gig.

XXXVIII

Despite the praise he got
and following of fans
Bird was a lonely soul.
de Koenigswarter tells:
'One night I saw him stand
out in the pouring rain.
Shocked, I asked him why.
"No place to go" he said.
"Often I use friends' pads
and doze in their armchairs
but none was home tonight.
Sometimes I ride subways
right to the terminus
then when they throw me out
I take another train
and ride it back again."'

XXXIX

Once at a party said
'Bartok and gin we have.
We need nothing else.'

XL

At his first Paris gig
a fan gave Bird a rose.
On finishing his set
Charlie waved that flower
to all the audience,
kissed it, ate it up,
all petals, stem and thorns.

XLI

Tutty Clarkin said:
'He often joined the band
after eight doubles downed
and frequently would drink
first a bottle of gin
and then a bottle of scotch
and he had ulcers then.
What I saw him take
would kill the average cat.
It killed him in the end.'

XLII

'When I drink too much
can't even finger well
far less play ideas'
Bird said to Teddy Blume.
The latter marvelled at
Parker's fortitude
who brilliantly performed
when full of benzedrine
or with eight doubles juiced
or after one big fix
still playing like a champ.

XLIII

Bird's sporadic cash
was squandered every day
in spite of joint and fix
admirers gave him free.
When he unrolled his sleeve
his arms were needle-marked.
He touched one scar and said
'There is my Cadillac'
and of another vouched
'This one is my house.'
The doctor at his death
found nowhere to inject
as all veins had been used.

XLIV

Sonny Rollins swore
that Bird assisted him
when he most needed it
as lately he was hooked
and Bird though hooked himself
still firmly disapproved
of any use of drugs
by clever younger men.
As Sonny looked to Bird
and thought him an ideal
it was Bird's impetus
made Sonny Rollins free.

XLV

When Walter Bishop asked
how he got hooked on dope
Bird gave him this account:
'Bish, there are many things
that have gone wrong with me.
I'd hire a specialist
and give a hundred bucks
for him to check my heart.
Don't do no good at all.
My heart is still messed up.
I see this ulcer man
and seventy five I pay
to cool my ulcers out.
Don't do no good at all.
My ulcers they still hurt.
But round a dismal lane
there lurks a little cat
and five bucks is his fee
for one small bag of shit.
Ulcer's gone, heart trouble gone,
my ailments gone away
and that is why I'm hooked.'

XLVI

Said Gerry Mulligan
although guys were about
who got around their horns
no one improvised
with more command and drive,
so fluid an ability
and such a sheer dexterity
as Parker with his horn.

XLVII

Jimmy Raney asked
'What is it that you think
while playing on the stand?'
'All troubles disappear
while working out a theme
when I blow my horn.'

XLVIII

The alto Gigi Gryce
heard Bird would visit stores
and seeing music there
would not buy a sheet.
His photographic mind
recorded every note.
He studied it awhile
then had it memorized
and found the shortest means
with his own fingering
to richly complicate.
Lent a horn by Gryce
he wailed away with it,
his hearers gassed for hours.

XLIX

Jimmy Forrest bought
three bright and fancy shirts
(each cost him fifteen bucks)
and laid them on his bed.
Bird coming in remarked
'Those three shirts sure are nice.'
At this poor Jimmy smiled
so glad that Bird approved.
'Which of them is mine?'
Bird asked his anxious friend
and seizing on the best
with it he disappeared.

L

Bird joined a game of golf
to make a threesome up.
He brought a fifth of scotch,
soda and some ice
squeezed into caddy carts.
The bass man had a bag,
not clubs but reefer stuff.
They found it hard to hit
the wayward ball at all
but liked the open air
and then the nineteenth hole.

LI

Each week Bird called his mom
from where he chanced to be,
once phoning in a storm
and when the thunder crashed
hung out the telephone
with a question on his lips:
'Do you hear God talking, Mom?'

LII

Once at a Harlem dance
whose theme was fancy dress
Bird as an alto went
not wearing anything
except a saxophone.

LIII

Bird once asked a friend
how much his wallet held.
The man replied: 'Five bucks.'
'Then let me take your bread.
I'll pool it all with mine.'
He put down thirty cents
then picked up the whole pile
and poured it in his purse.
They reached the Bowery
and then they grabbed a bum.
Bird punched him in the gut
and said they were police.
As the wino clutched his paunch
down into his shirt
Bird thrust their total sum.

LIV

Passing a bistro once
Bob Reisner saw a guy
ejected from its door.
Bird was that angry man.
He was obstreperous.
Ironic that he went
just as its juke box played
a record that was his.
With his solo pouring forth
they tossed him in the street.

LV

Would often sport a roll
so thick would choke a horse
or twirled around the keys
for a brand new car
but often scuffled for
a single silver Jeff.

LVI

To Harvey Cropper: 'Harv
you and me might split.
I might lose all my friends
but this I always have'
embracing his bright horn.
'This one is mine' exclaimed,
went off repeating this
hugging and kissing it.

LVII

There were so few could match
Bird on his instrument—
on trumpet Fats Navarro
and Max Roach on his drums
with Bud Powell on piano.
They made a dream quartet
if all had played as one.

LVIII

Max Roach likened Bird
to solar energy.
'We drew our warmth from him.
We're drawing on it still.
In all things musical
his ideas bounded out
and this inspired each one.
Bird had a playful means
that raised each instrument.
Strong on invention he
would write out one part first—
it was the trumpet one—
with all those funny rhythms.
He carefully wrote down
the different melodies,
transposed them to his horn
spelling the changes out
to bassist, pianist.
He'd look at me. I'd say
"What do I have to do?"
He'd say "You know that well."
He told me nothing more.
I guess he wanted me
to solve things for myself.'

'I wrote a tune one time.
"Night Train" was its name'
Jimmy Forrest said.
'Play your song' Bird asked.
'So we began to play
and when it came his turn
Bird played the hell from it
but when my turn approached
unable to go on
I said in compliment
"After you're through with it
what is there left to play?"
Quickly Bird replied
"That's one of the nicest things
that has been said to me."'

LX

Too often he was late
or absent from his stands
so juiced out, zombied, zonked
by the god of benzedrine
or genie in cocaine
or too sharp kick from horse
that he would doze all day
and long into the night.

LXI

Once horn beneath his coat
at the door began to blow,
continued to the stand
not taking his coat off.
Another famous time
when Lewis (Baby Face)
yelled 'Take it, Charlie Parker'
the spotlight swung on Bird
in his chair sound asleep.

LXII

Reviewing Parker's life
Budd Johnson reminisced:
'He had much love, respect.
I've seen him going up
to a group of strangers, say
"The night is growing cold.
I need an overcoat"
and glad to help him out
they catered for his need.'

LXIII

'Always Bird would treat
but if he had no cash
which often was the case
he'd treat us anyhow.
I saw one episode.
He'd ordered drinks for friends
at Birdland one wet night
and for his own dire thirst
three triple Grand Dads drank.
When asked to pay he said
"Give me a pen to write..."
When told cash was required
with the barman in pursuit
he quickly exited.'

LXIV

Buddy de Franco traced
what Bird had to the full,
an ideal sense of swing
but not for the gut alone.
There's also intellect.
Cerebral is the word
to echo in the mind.

LXV

André Hodeir said
Bird's supreme reform
was working into jazz
a new melodic line
so discontinuous
yet snaking in and out,
coherent all the time.
You always felt the tune,
Bird knowing where he was
however intricate.

LXVI

Bird's idea of rhythm
entails time broken up,
the accents so displaced,
on only half notes based,
those notes that other cats
diminished or ignored.
To Bird alone they were
both meat *and* gravy jazz.

LXVII

Accentuation comes
alternately on beats
or in between them falls
and so the rhythms dance.
Each hearer has to guess
but after long delays
and so much hanging on
resolves in all our ears
for our gratified response.

LXVIII

Changing from F to C
Dizzie or Monk or Bird
would play these complex lines
which no one else could play:
ninths augmented, flattened,
elevenths, diminished chords
which Ravel, Mahler, Bach
Debussy, Wagner, Liszt
had thought out to extend
music to all sound.

LXIX

One splendid night Bird blew
so many choruses—
they numbered twenty-five.
The tune was 'Cherokee.'
It was his favorite,
the one in which he learned
to make each tune his own.
He played it one whole week
each evening differently.

LXX

Bird gave some good advice:
'Don't reach the bandstand babe
with quarrels on your mind.
As a pulpit treat the stand.
As for your differences
leave them in the crowd
until you're at the end.
Resume your differences
only on coming down.'

LXXI

Bird said to Sonny Criss
'Don't think. Quit thinking now.
Rely on intuition.
To play is more than mind.'
When Criss heard Bird and Prez
conversing each to each
through their instruments
his observation was
'Man, it was outa sight.'

LXXII

As Bach's inventions show
you only need two voices
to make sound tapestries
and all the range of colors
imparting complex feelings
to any chord or series
so Prez and Bird in jamming
were two yet many voices.
Orchestral was their sound.

LXXIII

Together Bird and Diz
decided what to do
evoking with their horns
a double-headed man
one guy when they played
one guy with two heads
and not two horns but one.

LXXIV

Bird took a touch from Diz
Diz borrowed bits from Bird
together sharing much
each as a catalyst
to the other's artistry
so what they then produced
was doubly better than
what either made alone.
They were in unison.
It was a partnership.

LXXV

But blood was in their eyes
when both together went
to play upon the stand.
It was competitive,
each trying to extend
his partner into moves
which he could follow up,
try to consolidate
yet both the music shared
until they moved beyond
what formerly they did
when Diz outbirded Bird
and Bird outdizzied Diz.

LXXVI

At his new studio
Dizzie worked away
at home avoiding noise
as rooms were hard to find
refraining after dark
from playing trumpet parts.
'At three a.m. our bell
rang loudly. I unlocked
far as the chain extends.
A man was standing—Bird
holding his shining horn.
"Diz, let me in. I've got
this number in my head.
At last I've worked it out."
Putting down Bird's tunes
was something that I did.
Patience is what he lacked.
"Why can't you wait" I said,
"tomorrow's time enough."
'Tomorrow is too late.
By then I will forget.
Please, Diz. It's clear in mind."
I shut the door in his face.
He put his horn to mouth
playing his new tune.
On the other side I stood
and wrote the music down.'

LXXVII

Teddy Reig attests
that once Bird had to keep
a record date with Diz
but lolled within his tub
nearing the crucial time
and tried to sober up.
'Knowing well our man
we all went to his room,
broke in the bathroom door,
grabbed him from the tub,
dried him, dressed him up,
conveyed him in a cab
to the appointed place
just at the time arranged,
thrust his horn in his hands
and pushed him from the wings
out into center stage.
For its speed and new ideas,
selective artistry
the record they both made
was unbelievable.'

LXXVIII

'Bop City in San Fran
was a place for after hours
where jazzmen could relax
and jam away their time'
said Jerome Richardson.
'Once in '52
Bird was there though drunk.
We asked him to perform
with only a rhythm section
but it was powerful:
Art Blakey was on drums
with Kenny Drew on keys
and Curly Russell bass
but all were miffed at Bird
as he had messed them up
for bread on their last date.
They looked for their revenge. '

LXXIX

'"Choose any theme," he said.
It was '52nd Street.'
They started it so fast
that he was all tied up
with false starts, fingerings.
He stuttered twice then stopped.
"Give me an hour" he said
and in an hour came back,
took up his horn and played.
There was in all the world
no tune too fast or slow
or unfamiliar.
All night he played that horn.
The time passed like a dream.
We heard him into dawn.
He had blown away the dark.'

LXXX

Art Tatum shared with Bird
a downtown spot one night
with solo after solo.
When Charlie's turn was done
Tatum started up.
Bird listened a few minutes
so moved by what he heard
that he stepped up to the stand
and played with Art until
they put the tune they played
through every change they could.

LXXXI

Some who heard Bird play
recoiled from his exposure,
sheer rawness of emotion,
discomfort and neurosis
yet those who heard more clearly
and knew the things he blew
found full release in knowing
all their anxieties
were soothed by his clear horn.

LXXXII

At a famous club one night
down in the kitchen Bird
was carving sandwiches
until the manager
warned him he was on.
Bird sat before his plate
to the chagrin of his boss
who begged him tearfully:
'The crowd is restless now.'
Still munching them Bird said
'Man, try these sandwiches.
They're really crazy, man.'

LXXXIII

Bird taught Bob Newman horn.
'The fee each class a fin.
Except odd breaks for drinks
they took all afternoon.
His first instruction was
"Blow *through* your horn. *Play loud*..
Open your whole throat."
He urged me to control
vibrato with the mouth.
Vibrato was for Bird
from far back in the tongue.
Most teachers would agree
it is tabu to play loud
but a man with horn, Bird felt,
should make his statements strong.
"Blow through your horn as if
you were blowing a candle out."
Just then he only played
his special plastic horn.
He used a reed so stiff
I didn't even get
a single peep from it.'

LXXXIV

When he took up his horn
found something to explain
and needed you to guess
what he was thinking of.
A blare on sax would show
a woman on his mind,
one poignant minor key
illusions there in love
for music is a game
made individual
and a conversation with
each person in the crowd.

LXXXV

Just like Varèse he heard
music within all sound
reflecting on his horn
swish of a speeding car
dire siren of the cops
ready to make a bust
hum of the wind through leaves
Popeye's deep-toned voice
Olive Oyl's high pitch
falsetto in complaint.

LXXXVI

He played all colors too—
orange yellow green
all forty shades of blue
as if he played this for
every blue there was.
Red may raise the heart
and green redeem the world
especially in spring
but blue expresses soul,
the hunger each of us
has for the her or him
who rests there deep within
making of each a whole.

LXXXVII

So generous with tunes
Bird loaned to other cats
that sometimes they would steal
and pass off as their own
and when it came to style
so hard to copyright
(so Tristano said)
Bird could have sued the world
for plagiarism if
his improvising form
had been sufficient grounds.

LXXXVIII

Bird asked for five C-notes
from Oscar Goodstein once
in lieu of royalties.
'No deal. I'll give a fin.'
'Three hundred make it then.'
Two sawbucks Oscar gave.
Then Charlie saw a man
was needing a square meal
and gave his twenty bucks
so he could eat his fill.

LXXXIX

Those who copied him
or tried to imitate
were Sonny Stitt, Phil Woods,
Cannonball Adderley,
Ornette Coleman too
for imitation is
sincerest form of praise
and any one of them
was dying to achieve
what Bird alone could do.

XC

An episode Earl Hines
remembered many years,
when studying a tune
something entirely fresh
deciding to play that night,
all had a score but Bird
who sat apart at the end.
'I asked him "Had he seen?"
"Sure, Earl, I know it well."
"You've only seen it once.
Surely that's not enough."
"Once is enough for me.
I have it memorized."
Came evening he just played
the whole thing perfectly.'

XCI

Up front went Willie Jones
to play a final set.
He was a neophyte.
As everyone held on
for Bird to call the tune
an anxious Willie prayed
'not fast, man, not too fast'
for he had yet to learn
tempos he later played
rapidly with ease.
'52nd Street'
was the theme that Charlie chose,
its tempo ultra fast.
Jones scuffled his way along
unable to keep pace,
playing instinctively.
He was afraid to stop,
not wanting to be shown
for the novice that he was.
Ending, he went to Bird:
'Man, sorry for dragging it.'
'I did it to help you' was
Charlie's grave response.
Jones translated this:
'When you hit the stand you must
be ready for anything.'

XCII

Bird hearing Ella said
'It's good you don't play horn
for if you did it would
take all our jobs from us.'

XCIII

The Duke's lead trumpeter
Harold Baker felt
that all Bird wished to do
was live to play that horn.
'An eleventh was his start
or key's far thirteenth note
in sixteenths, thirty-seconds,
three times as fast on horn
as any other cat,
knew what he wished to play
before a finger moved.
So many guys forget
the changes they would make.'

XCIV

'Bird could ramble but
he got back to the key.
I never heard so fast
as that which Charlie played.
Fast as it was, it's clean,
band playing the tune straight.
They're giving Bird ideas.
They keep on feeding him.
He's chalking all the way.'

XCV

Once astride a horse
in central N.Y.C.
Bird tried hard to ride
down Charlie's Tavern steps.
He did it for a bet.

XCVI

Once dressed in dungarees
suspenders and bright shirt
just like a Kansas hick
in front of Birdland stood
and spoke to passers by
if they were smartly dressed:
'A jazz cat I presume.'

XCVII

Someone asked him why
he played the fool so much.
Gravely he replied
'It is my way to show
that people cheat themselves
in judging someone's worth
by pigment in the skin
and not by heart or mind.
The only way we have
to mock our foolishness
is make a joke of it.'

XCVIII

'What angers most' he said
'is poverty and want.'
He came to bed one night.
A man was on the floor
fast sleeping whom he slapped.
Surprised, the guy awoke.
Bird handed him five bucks
so he could rent a room
and rest in bed that night.

XCIX

They say he never wept,
was taught men should not cry.
Like all professionals
he could control his pain
but when his daughter died
(was just a baby still,
had hardly learnt to walk)
the way he shed his tears
was through his horn alone.

C

He vented all his rage
at what white did to black
over the centuries
remembering Bessie Smith
denied an ambulance
by the roadside left to die
because her skin was dark
and a million incidents
degrading to *all* men
when travelling below
and also far above
the Mason-Dixon line.

CI

Charlie Mingus tells
that Bird once came to him,
said suddenly 'Drop dead!'
Mingus, taken aback,
said 'Charlie, why say that?'
A smiling Bird replied
'Because you want to die.'
Mingus admitted that
just then he was depressed
and Charlie sensed his mood.
'Then would you die for me?
I'd surely die for you'
was all that Parker said.

CII

'Bird brought to music strains
I'd only heard before
in Beethoven's quartets,
Stravinsky even more'
Mingus once observed
terming Bird 'King Spook'
because of sleepless nights
when Parker endlessly
played upon his horn
with records backing him
over the telephone.

CIII

Walter Williams was a friend.
Williams could recall.
this trivial incident:
'Near dawn at 5 a.m.
I heard my doorbell ring.
I wondered who it was,
not someone in distress
as there's five flights to climb
so called "Who's there?" No sound.
Once open Bird stood there.
"Got a match?" he asked.
When I gave him it
he lit a cigarette
and went without a word.'

72

CIV

Robert Reisner notes
that things went well one night,
the people drifting in
glued to their seats by Bird
when at the interval
two shabby men came out
and started country crap.
When Reisner tackled them
they said Bird hired them both
to fill this interlude.
When questioned Bird agreed.
With arm on shoulder laid
to Reisner he explained:
'You do not understand.
We're full. These cats are bad
so some of the people leave.
Turnover's what we need.'
'Some con man you must be
providing all this hype
to fans who love you so.'
'Bobby' Bird replied
'Bread is your only friend.'

CV

Howard McGhee once said
'Whoever plays with Bird
feels that he's playing shit
to what Bird's putting down.'
The converse is as true.
Bird drove and he inspired
each man who played with him.
They rose above themselves.

CVI

Red Rodney knew this too.
'I was scared to death
but when he worked with me
that gave me confidence.
All told it from my play
accomplished in two weeks
and Bird did that for me.'

CVII

When asked by poet friends
'You dig the *Rubaiyat*?'
a grin was on his face
as he cited these four lines:
"Come, fill the Cup, and in the fire of Spring
Your Winter-garment of Repentance fling:
The Bird of Time has but a little way
To flutter—and the Bird is on the Wing."

CVIII

Like artists all world-wide
he loathed hypocrisy
and all bureaucracies.
On questions of what faith
Bird described himself
'musician' and 'devout.'
This was his one belief.
If art an artist trusts
he does not need a faith
or other human shams.

CIX

His records are delight.
Drop them to half the pace
just 16 r.p.m.
shows perfect little schemes,
each structure filling out.
Premeditated yet
it seemed spontaneous.

CX

Bird made his testament:
'Music is your world
your inner self, your soul,
and if you cannot live it
it won't come from your horn.
All professors teach you
music has its limits
but, man, we best remember
music is the spirit
transcending everything.'

CXI

'Regrettably just then
he was drinking to excess
downing a fifth each day
so juiced he barely played'
Dizzie Gillespie said
and then he spoke to Bird.
"Stan Kenton has a man,
Lee Konitz is his name.
All give him a big hand.
You taught him how to play
but you're letting down your fans.
You nothing say when juiced
and slobber on the horn.
You don't know what you do.
Kenton Konitz stars
because that man can play.
Bird, put that whiskey down!"
That night upon the stage
I rued I criticized
as I had to follow him.
He just ran snakes that night!'

CXII

Some months before Bird died
he told Art Blakey this:
'"Hear with your eyes" he said
"and see with your ears." It was
advice I can't forget.'

CXIII

Knowing like Falstaff that
he owed God one good death
in 1955
he never thought he'd live
to see that year begin
as health was worsening
but now maybe he'd reach
just half the Bible span.

CXIV

From Boston twenty miles
if you are driving west
is a place called Framingham.
Consider from its name
here there were Puritans
and here was Christie's club.
It overlooked a lake.
Loving the house and grounds,
its solemn old world charm
Bird liked to play in this
within a separate wing.
The men accompanying
played in another room.
Here he blew his best,
his horn at its most relaxed
in an introspective mood
where he could meditate
on the brevity of life,
on fortune and his fate.

CXV

Varèse of the avant-garde
had settled in New York.
Bird sought his tutelage.
'Accept me as a child
and teach me all you know.
I write in just one voice.
I want to understand
the inner worlds of sound
and to score for orchestra.
I'll pay you what you wish.
I make a lot of cash.'
So persistently he asked
that finally Varèse
agreed to take him on
and teach him all he knew.
When he returned to France
asked Bird to wait until
he came back after Lent.
But Charlie didn't last.
He died in early March.

CXVI

Some weeks before he died
was strolling on Broadway
and had but fifty cents
when he saw a blind man play
on his accordion.
Bird dropped into his cup
a quarter from his sum
(a half of what he had)
and asked the guy to play
'All The Things You Are.'
Several minutes passed
and then when Bird returned
the man continued with
the number Charlie asked.
At this Bird laughed and said
as he took his last two bits
and placed them in the cup
'This boy with all his skill
makes every change just right.'

CXVII

Frank Sanderford confessed
the last time he saw Bird
was at the Beehive Club
(Chicago was the place)
as the owner needed help
to get poor Charlie on.
'Seated in a room
used only to store beer
Bird came and greeted me
as if I truly were
the only friend he had.
The house was overfull
and expectation high.
Everyone had come
to hear how he would play.
He was too sick to play.
I should have noted this,
not tried to get him on.'

CXVIII

'"They came to see" he growled
"the junky who was crowned
most famous in the world."
I'll always feel the guilt
at getting him to go
unsteady to the stand.
To mouth he lifted horn,
blew in the embouchure.
It made a few sad sounds,
a bleating like a goat.
He could not play at all.
He was a beaten man.
He died soon after this.'

CXIX

A week before he died
he hummed to Sonny Stitt
'I give you the kingdom's keys,
those keys to the kingdom, man.'

CXX

'Do you drink?' the doctor asked
when slumped in pain he lay.
He said with sidelong wink
'An aperitif at lunch
to give an appetite.'

CXXI

Bird uttered his last words
as he watched a music show:
'What a wonderful trombone!'
Praise was on his lips
praise that was musical
when drawing his last breath.
He then began to choke
while laughing at an act
and fell back in his chair.
'I phoned immediately'
said the baroness.
'He slipped away just then.
I felt his pulse. It stopped.
I knew that Bird was dead.'

CXXII

'As the moment passed
there came a thunderclap.
Just then I hardly knew
but now I think, "How strange!"'
When this they heard some said
'Was God receiving Bird
or Bird knocking at the Gate?'

CXXIII

Bird died aged thirty-four
yet he looked fifty plus.
The year was '55
the day was March the twelfth
eight forty five the hour
with New York not long dark.
All light had left the world
when Charlie Parker died.

CXXIV

There were quarrels at his will
by two of several wives
but the second, Geraldine,
had had enough of him
to last her her whole life
but wittily she said
in that true Parker style
'A horn was all he had
when I married him,
a horn and one great vice.
As he gave that vice to me
his horn I want to have.'

CXXV

The tributes flooded in:
this character devised
the means for modern jazz;
in all keys Bird played well
and every tempo too;
on horn three times as fast
as any other man;
would never patterns lose,
knew what he wished to play
before a finger moved;
but many mourning fans
adoring the whole man
on sidewalk and on wall
wrote in their faith: 'Bird Lives!'

Glossary

The Baroness: Baroness Pannonica de Koenigswarter, jazz
      patroness
Bop: music characterized by syncopation in which the beat
      precedes the melody, wind and wood instruments
      playing in a flat tone, the use of short double and
      triple notes replacing longer notes, sudden changes
      in the octave or register, and sudden changes in key
      and rhythm, sometimes accompanied by scat lyrics.
Bread: money
C-note: hundred dollar bill
Cat: a jazz musician
Changes: the harmonic progression (that is, the series of
harmonies) of an existing theme (often a popular song) on
which a jazz performance is based.
Chip: to use drugs sporadically
Dig: understand, approve, enjoy
Double tempo: twice as fast
The Duke: Duke Ellington, bandleader
Ella: Ella Fitzgerald
Embouchure: part of musical instrument applied to mouth
Ensemble: concerted passage in which all performers unite
Fifth: one fifth of a U.S. gallon
Fin: five dollar bill
Fix: an injection of narcotics, especially heroin
Gassed: evoke an emotional response (in this sense the word
was first applied to Charlie Parker's playing)
Gig: jazz engagement or job
Grand Dad: drink comprising an ounce of Bourbon (three
      triple Grand Dads would amount to nine ounces of
      hard liquor)
H: heroin
Hick: farmer, farm hand
Hock: pawn
Horse: heroin

Hype: to cheat
Jamming: to extemporize
Jam session: group extemporization
Joint: marijuana cigarette
Juiced: intoxicated
Junky: someone hooked on narcotics
K.C.: Kansas City
Phillie: Philadelphia
Pipes: vocal chords, voice
Rap: arrest or jail sentence
Riff: short repeated phrase in jazz
Roy: Roy Eldridge, trumpet player
Sawbuck: ten dollar bill
Silver Jeff: a nickel
Take: to record on tape
Tristano: Lennie Tristano, jazz pianist
Two bits: twenty-five cents
Wail: improvise
Woodshed: to practise alone, from going off by oneself to
          the woodshed for intensive private practice
Yardbird: prisoner
Zombied: turned into a zombie, lose one's mental powers
Zonked: intoxicated